{ The Coder Habits }

—

The #39# habits of the professional programmer

—

Rafael Gómez Blanes

2020

English first edition – October 2020 - #01#
Rafael Gómez Blanes - Copyright © 2020
All rights reserved
The Coder Habits: The 39 Habits of the Professional Programmer
www.rafablanes.com
ISBN: 9798698479406

To my parents, my sister and daughters,
Luna and Beatriz

To my spouse

To all my Solid Stack partners

Index

{ Introduction }

—

If I had to resume the reason some people are doing better than others, personally and professionally, I would say that what makes the difference between are their habits.

Habits regarding health, financial issues, relationships and even your own inner dialogue. And, of course, also their professional habits.

Since I am a computer engineer and coder and I work in the software industry since longer than I can remember, I want you to come with me through the following pages and learn what distinguishes the best professionals and those who have better results than the rest.

I have reflexed a lot about this topic to come to the conclusion that a good professional becomes one because they mix indisputable technical skills with the needed habits and daily routines and the way they understand their profession.

So, you may consider yourself a great coder but if you do not have other skills (more than those you can imagine for starters) that I tell you about in this job, you are putting yourself obstacles in your career and your progress capacity.

Since the first draft of this book, I have collated my conclusions with most of my experiences (good and bad), just to confirm them with greater vehemence and conviction.

A habit consists in doing a certain deed you have interiorized in such a way that, simply, you do it automatically and, what's even better, with no effort.

Add some positive habits and your life will get better, live with negative habits and you will find yourself in a lot of trouble: personally, as well as professionally.

I barely trust willpower; this force, if it truly exists, so exalted and always referred to as the main motor to do all that is important to do, it barely lasts a little while every day; let's say that each morning, when your alarm bells and see the first light of day from your room's window, you start the day with a very limited supply of what they call "willpower". That's why it is always recommended to do the tasks we like the less first or that are harder to do, in the morning, when we are not exhausted yet.

You will not have success with an iron willpower, no matter what you call success. It is better and easier to collect positive habits that lead you directly there and just discard the negative habits. Leave willpower aside and focus on habits.

Simple, but not easy.

For some reason, in this moment of my life, I find it easy to wake up earlier to do yoga before starting the work day, writing a list of my daily tasks each morning, going out for a daily one-hour walk, writing at least 1000 words a day, run tests as something natural in my job and dedicate hours to plan and organize. A long time ago, all those activities, that are certainly, positive and desirable, were hard to me, now I do them easily. Why? Because I managed to turn them into habits.

I have spent years studying anything related to them, maybe seeing that the key to have a better life was there, with amazing readings that I include in the bibliography. All the authors that write about it, they coincide that they are a powerful tool in our brain to save energy, no more, no less.

If you think about it, it makes all the sense in the world: when you do a task, over and over again, our brain ends up saving the instructions for doing it, until you do it with no effort, now we do it almost without blinking and automatically.

Think about it: it was very hard for me to learn how to drive, in a year, I was driving perfectly. The same thing happens with any other activity or skill that is somehow difficult and requires some certain number of repetitions to get to do it every time better, from playing an instrument, drawing and cooking to more mundane tasks like hanging a picture or painting a wall.

And also programming and running a software project.

That's it, you can incorporate habits in your daily life that will allow you to code better and improve as a professional.

I have written a lot about why software projects fail, a topic I touched in "The Black Book of the Programmer" (#1 in Amazon sales in its category a lot of times), also about the good practices a professional coder has to have to write a sustainable high-quality code in "The Practical Book of the Agile Programmer", and I have even synthesized in a simple method the agile way of systematize the functioning, exploitation and improving of a project or business, with "The Lean MP Method".

At the same time, I have observed how some coders do it good, professionally and even naturally, while others have it three times harder without even hardly meeting the quality of the first ones.

If you feel you are over compensating continuously day by day as a coder, that your results are mediocre or that they could improve, and that for some reason your performance is low and the code you are producing has a questionable quality, while you know someone who just seems to be blessed by some magic hand and everything they do turns out well, so I got news for you: you do not lack intelligence, you don't have to work double (not even read more technical articles), what makes you different from that person are just habits (technical and from other nature I describe in this book) and, apart from yours, are way better. That's it.

Writing good software is not only about knowing how to code, it isn't just a technical matter. As in any other activity, everything that turns around this job has an impact on it, from good organization to an adequate environment, positive group dynamics, good readings and a continuous attitude for improving.

Up next I describe what I have found and the conclusions I met after thinking a lot about the subject: a set of 39 habits that, being incorporated in your daily life, will make a change and get you to create better quality software, completing the projects more easily and being a better professional, without a doubt.

Consider those habits as authentic wisdom pills that will get you to the next level. Some of them are related to technical matters, but about half of them are routines and attitudes that impact your work and some of them will certainly surprise you.

Also, I decided I will not take too much of your time, so each habit will be written in the quickest, simplest way possible, going straight to the point but allowing you to grow your curiosity and, if you wish, dig deeper in those that attract you the most. That's why I also share my preferred bibliography at the end of the book.

This is that I propose you: multiply your results as a professional with a lot less effort. How?

With more and better habits.

{ #1 - Apply the 50/50 rule }

—

We believe that coding consists in just writing «new» code. This is, that we only «ruly» work when we add a new functionality and characteristics, which is, maybe, the funniest part for some.

This is a belief that is somehow naïve from those who have not understood the nature of launching a professional project.

You will spend more time reviewing and modifying any code than writing it, so, probably, what you had in the beginning has little or nothing to do with what you will have in the following months.

I have observed this: when you have little experience, you try to spend most of the time writing new code; however, the more time you have spent in the profession, the more you enjoy improving the solution. Weird, but it has an explanation.

If you do not stop adding new code and don't stop to check what you wrote, you will be making mistakes and repeating them, the technical debt you left behind will affect you sooner or later. The «technical doubt» are all those «to-do's» that you have to improve and those things that are not quite good (maybe you are not aware of it yet). When you amass more and more technical debt, the more effort you will have to invest in correcting it, in fact, the difficulties grow exponentially.

I call this the «50/50 rule», it is a way of describing that we have to spend half of our time writing new code (in the form of new functionality and its tests) and the other half reviewing it and improving it (cleaning and design). Both activities are part of what we call «coding». This percentage is an estimate, of course, but what is important to note is that we have to dedicate a good amount of time in improving and refactoring, continuously, and that job is inescapable in our daily basis.

It is true that we often work under deadlines and with a certain development method that imposes some times and the characteristics we have to develop and modify, so we will often meet pressure that makes us add functionality and put aside any other thing that involves improving what is already there. Doing this on the run and at any price, could suppose a shot to our own feet.

We have to reach some balance between both activities and the deadlines we agreed on, and we should also understand that any time used to improve some aspect of what is already there and works, will facilitate our job when adding some new functionality and we will spend less time doing so, so improving the code and its design is in the end, an investment and not a waste.

If you can, it is a good idea to dedicate some effort to that improving job when beginning a new development or «sprint» phase, as a way of cleaning and preparing the way for the new functionality you will add.

Also, actively making this improving job, will allow you to polish the code as much as you can and get to a point in which it is all well-designed and coded, that, over time, you will learn some things that will improve your initial code more and more; you do not get to learn all those things when you do not put any time in thinking what to improve and how, but only correcting bugs and keeping the initial code untouched because you think you «already invest too much time on it», and that modifying it could suppose throwing away part of this effort. But that's very far from truth.

Continuously improving the project is a good habit that will facilitate and improve your life as a developer.

You may be asking yourself that if you continuously touch the code to improve it, what assures you that it is still running correctly? With an amply battery of tests, units, integration, etc. There's nothing more. It is obvious but, do you do it?

If you find yourself with some free time, you do not want to read at the moment, what to do? A micro-improvement, adding more and better tests, etc. There is always something to improve in a software project.

Think what would happen if you accumulate a hundred micro-improvements over weeks and thousands over months.

{ #2 - Learn something new every week }

—

If you do not progress, it is because you're going backwards. That's it.

You may feel comfortable doing exactly the same things year by year: working on the same type of project, always using the same type of solutions, in the same environment and using the same language.

I want to tell you that that environment and language, are obsolete since longer than you can imagine, not in vain, the software industry is one of the more dynamic out there because all the economy is migrating to digital, if it hasn't done it yet somewhere. And I am not talking about fixed webs like a publicity issue, but technologies that were very expensive before and nowadays anyone can possess them (like all services brought by the cloud computer platforms), solutions that were so expensive are now open to be used at a very competitive price, new coding environments with very specific projects and allow new professions to exist like data scientists, big data analysts, security analysts, etc.

Now you can sell a project over the world in a wide range of «marketplaces» and «stores» and if you do not know how to do something you can just take a look to a similar project in GitHub.

If you think that all this new wave will not affect you over the next 10 years of your career, you may be approaching the sector in a very naïve way.

Yes, there are still places using VBA, Delphi and Objective C, but they are the exception rather than the rule.

Our profession demands us, even more than others, to continuously learn and leave behind the knowledges that are no longer useful, and not only regarding technical matters, according to your role, we still have to improve some personal skills, equipment management and leadership, improve our communication skills, learn about marketing and who knows what else we might need.

It may seem exhausting, but actually it consists in a continuous job and keeping an eternal beginner attitude, being willing to learn. You should also have the habit of reading an article here and there, reading the newsletters you receive from your subscriptions to be up to date on the topics you are interested in, reading a good book every once in a while, etc.

Also, never information and learning were as accessible as now.

I do not think that the professional who has read thousands of articles, hundreds of books, went to dozens of seminars and webinars and worked in ten different projects will be the same who has done nothing of the sort. The first will progress and multiply their employability, the second..., well, they should buy a lottery card for Christmas and hope for the best (R.I.P.).

{ #3 - Know and use data structures and algorithms correctly }

Programming, in essence, consists on manipulating data one way or another: data that is stored in a data base or any other type of repository, that are analyzed and manipulated to obtain a result (business logic), that are structured in a way that adds some certain value, etc. Surely, at a very basic level, there is always a set of data in which you apply some sort of algorithm.

However, and away of any academic theory, it is common to find applications that make a certain management of its data entities in a plain way and apply some very sequential type of logic, that is, their entities lack of structure and its processing is based on an «if» this, and therefore «if» that, therefore...

The coding art consists in reducing the problems to solve in classic data structures and well-known algorithms applied over them. It is surprising its absence in many applications.

Not in vain, in plain 1976, Niklaus Wirth wrote a book that became a reference in the incipient software industry and the title «Algorithms + Data Structures = Programs».

The problem is that we often code without trying to fit what we have to solve in the data structure and algorithms that runs it; in such a way, we reinvented the wheel and solved the problems as we think about them.

To set a few examples, sometimes you used an «array» when in reality you have to use a list or a certain type of «stack» data or «fifo» or «lifo» queues, unique identity markers you are in charge of generating when you could just use a «hash», applying for «whatever» to find out there are not repeated elements on a list when you should use some «unique set», the same way, you complicate yourself finding out the common elements in two «sets» when in reality it is about unifying them, and a big etcetera.

Priority queues, key/value lists, trees, graphs, dictionaries, cells, binary trees and many more, these are just some of the data structures that should be in your habitual vocabulary.

Likewise, linear or binary search algorithms, ordination like («mergesort», «quicksort», etc.), depth search (or DFS), «string pattern matching», «map/reduce» and many others, are algorithms that do not exist as a simple academic whim, but they rather help to resolve some typical computing problems, you may be developing and ERP, a website, a game or any other thing you can imagine.

It is true that many apps consist on a simple CRUD (creating, reading, updating and deleting data): user interface, some business logic and a data base to insert, delete or extract information; but many others, you can resolve things better by applying the right data structures and algorithms.

But please, do not invent your own ordination, search, chain validations, encryption methods. Learn the bases of this industry and just propose something new when you have something in your hands that is truly particular.

You got two arrays with chain identification, and you need to extract the ones appearing in the other two. Maybe you start iterate one first and then the other... the answer to the problem is nothing more than the intersection between two sets. If problem resolution you «think» from the data structure and classic algorithms, many will be solved in a more easy and elegant way.

{ #4 - Do not make the same mistake twice }

—

We always make mistakes; what may differ ones from the others is making the same mistake over and over again (which is a stubbornness symptom) and those you actively learn from their mistakes, problems and obstacles.

The first thing concurs with a proud character (trust me, this is a ballast in your personal and professional growth) and the second is always related to a humble personality and a bigger capacity of learning and improving. Choose the type of attitude you want to have.

I really do not mind making mistakes, even the people who are close to me know that I always admit the things I've done that did not work accordingly. But what I do not allow is to make the same mistake twice and I do anything I can to avoid it.

As software developers, we have a lot of ground for mistakes: design errors, selecting the wrong libraries, inefficient version and setting management, poor task distribution, underestimating time, scripts that are hard to keep, projects that are impossible to migrate to other environments, even a poor selection of work partners, etc., it's ok, and I will stop now because I am getting depressed.

Turning into a better professional is not about coding more and more in different environments learning each new technology without digging deeper on any of them (something I call «technological dilettantism»). A concept poorly learned is something you will poorly apply always, at any place and using any technology. It is smarter to do the humble exercise of recognizing what we do wrong and finding out what we can do to avoid doing so in the future.

If you know the same things as some years ago, when you follow the same paths and even use the same «tooling», then you have turned yourself in a petrified professional and with less room for improving and prospering. Don't say nobody told you so.

If you find the same problems in more than one project, if you hardly meet the deadlines accorded with the client, if you never deploy production without meeting critical errors and if you work in a team where stress is chronical, then you have some topics to learn (you and most probably your boss too). It is regrettable to believe that all this chaos is a core part of our activity. There are people who think that if you do not work under stress and with a problem mountain on your shoulders, then you are doing it wrong.

You can meet the deadlines comfortably, you can produce an impeccable, stable and error-free project, and you can also have a work team that is well-organized, with good planification and no stress; you just have to know how.

When facing any error, ask: what did it happen? What can I do to avoid this same mistake from happening again?

Ask the same questions before hundreds of different problems and you will become a much better professional.

This is about continuous improving.

I often make «retrospectives» when I reach some sort of peak and I always try to notice the problems that may appear, as long as they are new. For me, at least, this tactic has worked and maybe that is why I am capable of anticipating problems when I see some sort of subtle circumstances, whether they are technical as well as group dynamics and the relationships with clients.

It is not about age or experience, but having learned something from them.

{ #5 - Write readable code }

I have to admit that when developing a basic program, of any sort and on any environment, is something anyone can learn in just a few hours, with or without previous experience.

Writing software is, in essence, solving problems. Each kind, each method or each language function non-orientated to objects, solve «something» and they have a very clear purpose.

The ability consists on solving this problem in a simple way and, of course, a readable way, that is, easy to comprehend by anyone who takes that piece of code afterwards.

Simple, but not easy.

A good habit, yes, but we often forget it, especially when the deadlines are close (or we feel lazy to go and correct this or that).

It is weird that there are people who write code in a convoluted way on purpose, maybe trying to childly show-off their skills and techniques and inflate their ego, when, actually, it is about doing quite the opposite, and I have no doubt: the hard part is no longer about finding a simple solution to a problem, but expressing it in an equally simple way and, therefore, a more readable way.

I always say that writing software consists in a partnership and generosity act in each code line: what you are coding now, will probably be taken by a partner in the near-future. Why do you complicate their job?

Maybe you will be the one who will have to go back to the

method you expressed in such a dirty and hard to comprehend way, so you will be the one to blame, because you will take longer and need more effort to do it.

The solution? Make an effort to create code that is easy to read, even if that means writing code with a little less performance.

If you publish repositories in GitHub, you will have more success as long as those can be read, assumed and evolve for other people.

It is possible that you have a lot of experience coding and that you have a great amount of tricks in mind that you often use (split('-'.join('')), but remember to always write code that is not meant for you, but to be understood by others.

The more readable the code is, the more sustainable it will be.

How to write with more simplicity and transparency? That's what clean code techniques are for, as well as refactoring, «bad smells» detections you surely know, but, of course, a whole lot of experience in different projects and a lot of work and effort to continuously improve the work that's already done.

{ #6 - Start with the hardest (or the things you feel lazier to do) }

—

Coding, writing, planning and organizing, and any other creative task, requires a well-centered and motivated mind. We often procrastinate those tasks that we feel lazier to do (but that will be have to do anyway) and relegate them to the last moment; retarding the inevitable may be ok as long as you can afford it, but without a doubt, it is about a hard task or one that you don't find particularly appealing, you will have a constant mental purr reminding you what's left.

This constant reminder is annoying, and what's worst, it will ballast your concentration and motivation in the current moment. It often happens to me at the beginning of each semester when I have to gather the documentation for taxes and other fiscal obligations, and also when I have to run tests for projects, I finished some weeks ago, just to set a few examples.

For this reason, instead of delaying what I will have to do at some moment, many productivity techniques will tell me to get rid of them as soon as possible. When they're over, ahhhh, what a relief, now I can do what I truly like.

I have years doing this, that is, I start each morning making a list of all the tasks for the day (regarding job, my personal life and even domestic tasks), and always (or often, to be honest), I start doing what I like the less to later focus on what I find more stimulating or care more about.

But beware, later we will talk more about the best moment of the day to make what is less important, so you will always find a balance between getting rid of what you like the less and the adequate moment to do it.

Another tactic consists on doing all you don't like in a day just to be «clean» and work better the next day. You can clean (is a metaphor) every once in a while, and work without any annoying mental purr.

Your long-term goals have to be reduced to mid-term goals and, therefore, what you have to do is just decide what you will do every day. As simple as that, but it requires a great discipline and just avoid do anything just «when you feel like it».

That document that resists, that reunion your boss is waiting for, those tests you left uncomplete, that refactoring of a very dirty kind you finished last week, that other report your manager is asking for or those technical documents the offer guys had asked you about... whatever it may be, the less unpleasant tasks you have ahead, the more and better you will concentrate and the more calm you will feel while working, and it will without a doubt reflect in your better design decisions, better quality code and less errors and technical debt.

If you want to increase your productivity and concentration, start by finishing what you like the less first.

{ #7 - Type fluidly }

I feel some sort of trepidation writing about this, but sometimes you have to remember even the most obvious things.

I dearly remember a former boss of mine who spent more than 10 minutes writing a three-paragraph e-mail and he ended each day with tired eyes.

As IT professionals and coders, we spent a lot of our time working with a keyboard (what a surprise). Now I encourage you to make an investigation exercise and observe how your mates' type, and answer to those questions:

Do they type fast?

Is there someone who spends too much time going from the mouse to the keyboard and the same way around?

Do not tell me, please, but... is there someone who types using just their index fingers?

And lastly, do you feel identified with any of the questions above?

Forgive me if you feel attacked, I am just pointing out something important.

If you do not know how to type properly, your job is getting harder than necessary, because you will spend a lot more of time writing and making a lot of typographic mistakes and the «del» key will be the one you use the most.

This is something I was lucky at because when I was 13, a

summer when I felt particularly bored, I convinced my mother to sign me up for typing lessons (and it was in that same academy where I had my first contact with domestic computers, even before the PC era). Maybe that is why, even when using computers since such a young age, I still don't need glasses.

You have to learn how to use the keyboard with all the fingers of both hands (or almost all). I already mentioned this is pretty obvious, but ask yourself if your typing notions are correct.

If not, you need a quick course and I assure you that in just a month you will be staring only at the screen and you will be amazed at how you can write as fast as you speak multiplying your PPM (pulsations per minute). An excellent level consists in being able to write between 60 and 70 words per minute. With just 50 you are already among the best, which is just a 10%.

Seriously, as obvious as it may seem, it is important that you use your keyboard accordingly, and I am not talking about shortcuts in the operating system or text editor, but just about some minimum typing foundations.

{ #8 - Finish everything you start }

—

This is another one of the habits that you can apply to your professional life as well as your personal life.

We sometimes set objectives, challenges and goals, but don't get anywhere because we discourage from them at the first obstacle, lack of time or lack of motivation.

Our mind is pretty optimistic and ignores the long path of difficulties that any complex project has. Think of it this way: if there were no difficulties, someone else would already have done what you are proposing.

I discovered from my own experience that if you propose to just finish the things you decided to start some time, you will learn a lot of things among the way, more than you can imagine. Not in vain we often hear how what is important is the process, rather than the result. We fall in love with the last thing, without realizing that the first thing is the essence of any advance, whether it is personal or professional. You do not need to know it all to start, begin now and learn what you will need while doing it.

Many years ago, I was starting a lot of software projects and digital entrepreneurships. I did not finish most of them. Even more, I did not even reach ten percent of its development.

Over time I learned that I lacked compromise. No more, no less.

But I also understood that getting to the end was what really gave me knowledge, polishing my tenacity and enriching my technical knowledges. Leaving anything uncompleted gave me a lot of frustration and my self-esteem lowered.

Don't leave anything undone: that test battery you have to do, this important refactoring you know you have to do or that documentation that you know it could get better; do not ignore a problem because you find it hard to solve, understand that overcoming such difficulty will get you to learn how to solve such problems. Forget the word «problem» and consider it a «situation that needs a creative solution», also ignore even the «failure» concept, approach it as an improving result with which you have learned a lot.

If you always decant for the easy stuff, you will never learn anything important.

I believe there are better or worse professionals, just people who decided to face more problems or maybe, get out of that well-known and safe comfort zone. Both cases, it is alright, but each option has its advantages and obstacles.

However, you have to know that the bigger the challenge, the bigger the reward.

I learned more from those problems that caused me an authentic difficulty than those that I solved within minutes.

If you still haven't noticed, we turn into better professionals solving obstacles and overcoming difficulties (that's what we get paid for, actually), but we have to get to the end of it. Stop getting to some and you will soon turn into a technological dinosaur.

If you still do not understand it, it's because you haven't enjoyed the sensation of accomplishing your goals and you haven't tasted the pleasure of well-done work: there is nothing more gratifying than the kind words a satisfied client gives to your work, a gratitude e-mail from someone who has read your books thousands of miles away or the petition from someone in GitHub about a change because they want to use one of your repositories.

If it doesn't work, if you do not get the acknowledgement, the suitability or the reward you hoped from this project in which you invested lots of illusion and effort, that's alright. It is part of the game. What matters the most is the attitude of finishing it.

Then, you will see what happens.

I think I read the author of Candy Crush stating that before having success with this millionaire game, he published more than 50 games.

Fulfill your professional compromises and get to the end of your personal projects. The richness you need as a professional is on the way.

And if we get a little mystical, the thanatologists say that something many moribund people regrets is exactly that, «not giving it a try».

{ #9 - Apply design principles and patterns }

—

Software development, like any other industry with some certain maturity, it has advanced with the analysis of many failed projects and the conclusion that the monolithic software is impossible to evolve and change (maybe not impossible, but it is definitively less viable). However, you will find many current apps that are excessively monolithic made by many different companies.

It is possible to make any type of program and make it work, as much as I can build a little house without knowing nothing about architecture and barely having some masonry notions; but maybe, the walls of this house will not stand more than a few months so I wouldn't dare going inside.

Even in some corporative environments with million euros bills, I have found projects with no heads nor tails, poorly made, dirty, with no architecture and without those guides or well-known molds that are called «design principles» in software, and without those simple recipes that solve concrete problems called «design patterns».

Those principles are not an academic whim that just fit an environment free from the pressure of deadlines, but a safeguard for the code you are writing to e better structured, it is more understandable and, of course, easier and more flexible to change and that is more professional. If you still don't know it, it is in the software's nature to change when new requisites appear.

It doesn't matter the coding environment or the language you chose to use, most of those design principles and patterns can be applied at any time until you are so into them that you use them without knowing it.

S. O. L. I. D., KISS, Dependency Injection, Investment Control and many more principles just as Singleton, Façade, etc. and many other well-known patterns and documentation, that have to be in your programmer DNA, and precisely exist to make our live easier, the same way I commented before when I was talking about data structures and well-known algorithms. You choose to build a house by yourself without blueprints, without a technical rigger or an architect, and try to see what comes from it.

This is also a suitability issue: the better designed your project is, the easier and faster you will adapt it to the client's new requirements and it will be even harder to introduce errors. Without going any further, a product I designed and directed for a few years, thanks to its good design (easy, I have done some pretty awful things) we have been able to adapt it to other marketplaces, getting more clients at a lower cost.

You can take some licenses, of course: a project that you will deliver and never touch again, maybe you don't have to spend too much time polishing every detail of it, in such a case we should invest all the time we can doing a good design with the clear implementation in design principles.

{ #10 - Do not develop unsolicited characteristics }

A lot of programmers really enjoy what we do, very much, and we even get excited when we work on a project that we also like and we got to develop for some client. In some cases, we feel so close to them that we end up thinking we understand their business even more than they do.

Taking requirements is a complicated task, it consists in extracting the client's needs (if they know it 100% sure when they have a vague idea of what they want and how they want it), and translating those need to a more familiar language for developers.

This step should be done by someone who understands the client's context and also domains the language used by us, the developers; therefore, is an activity where it is easy to meet misunderstandings and requirements that, maybe are not as important for the client or have been explained wrongly. This is part of our daily life.

Nowadays, we know that the «functional analyst» role is still a hard to find chimere in most software enterprises.

Knowing this, it is even worse that some introduce characteristics that were not approved by the client or not even required just because they «think» the client will like them or will we useful.

Then we meet the cruel reality: the client rejects them and you find out that you have lost a lot of time (and money) doing something that will not be used.

In the context of a project that is realized for a third-party, all the implemented characteristics should be related to its needs, not to what we think it needs.

There are enough elements that could provoke deviations in the project just for us to introduce more.

Do not implement characteristics the client has not explicitly required and you have not even talked to them about those.

Proactivity is good, and those who work very much are always grateful that we propose ideas or possible solutions and improvements, we those have to be previously approached.

Imagine you hire a mason to do an ampliation of a room in your house, and one day you come home from work to see they have endorsed a stall in the middle of the garden, just because they thought it would be useful for you.

Don't put bricks where no one has asked you to.

{ #11 - Develop modular and flexible code }

—

Any app can be reduced to a set of parts (modules, libraries, components, etc.) that relate to one another to offer some functionality. If those parts are not properly differentiated, then we are talking about a «monolithic» app (inherited from the first complex programs that grew and grew sequentially and without structure), as we have pointed out previously.

The smaller and more isolated those parts are, the more «decoupled» the solution is, and this is not only good but desirable.

You find out your application is very coupled when you change something and, automatically, there are collateral errors that appear unexpectedly.

An app with a high level of decoupling allows you to work in a concrete module without affecting the rest, so it is easier to test and, if needed, a module could be substituted for a different version while the app remains built, functioning normally.

Try that every part of your app lives on their own independent world, serving the rest without depending of them.

A typical example is an application is totally linked to a certain type of data servers (MySql, Oracle, PostgreSgl, Sql Server, etc.) it would be impossible to change it for another (or it could be done at a high cost and with no control over the errors that would appear).

There are ways to avoid excessive decoupling through a good design thought to interchange parts of the app independently.

Designing the solution in such a way, it allows the reutilization of modules from some apps in others. Not in vain, the «componentization» of apps and the «microservice» architecture is what is desired.

Trying to modulate an app as much as possible and that each module is as independent as could be from the rest. You will know if you are doing it right when you check the effort of replacing or modifying the type of data bases, of ORM, of log mechanisms, of encryption libraries, of field validation or even the business logic itself, is minimum.

The longer the life of the app is intended to be and the more changes you would expect, the more emphasis you should put in making its coupling level extremely low.

I assure you I have seen true dramas because of this: systems that fed a whole business but with a coupling level so high that they had to be done again completely to allow them to evolve with new changes and new necessities within the same business.

{ #12 - Develop «soft-skills» }

—

A technician is not just a technician, a good professional is not only that person who does a complex job right. Don't think that in order to be a great coder, you only have to... know how to code. It is necessary but not enough.

Maybe you have realized it, but you always do work for someone else (whether you personally know them or not), and it is very probable you are integrated in a team among other people and you have to go to meetings with other profiles from your same company or with clients.

As much as you will find many recommended books in the bibliography, this section is a crash course about all those skills you should possess and enrich to become a better professional. Sadly, no one tells us about them in our academic stage.

As in any other profession, we interact with many other people, so we got to know how to «connect» with them, so, we should always put ourselves in each other's shoes; this is, you have to be empathic enough so your communication with other people results correct and efficient.

You should be able to communicate yourself correctly, and I am not only talking about, as if you are talking to your grandmother whom you love so much; communicating well is about going straight to the point, being correct in the modals and tone, launching important ideas at the beginning and not extend yourself more than intended and do not extend yourself more than necessary (taking other people's time). Those principles should be applied on earth, sea and air, I mean, if you communicate correctly when you write an e-mail, when you speak in public or when you redact a document for your company, a partner or a client.

At the same time, communicating well is a back and forth ride: listen to the other person with attention, do not interrupt and speak as clear as possible.

I have met amazing professionals (on the technical level) who were uncapable of doing team work. I always say: it is much better to have a qualified team of motivated people with «average» technical skills but with a team culture than having a team of gurus who are uncapable of working together.

A good professional knows how to work on a team and, therefore, works «inside the team» and «for the team», and whatever they do facilitates the work of the others, when they do not become an island just interested in information, when they're active during the meeting and supports a partner as much as they can.

This is the biggest challenge a manager faces: knowing how to create a homogeneous and compenetrated team.

You also become a better professional when you are not stubborn with your opinions and ideas, but are rather open to hear the ideas of others and even change your opinion as much as you need to, you may also be aware that it is not necessary to work extra time, but doing it creatively, and when problems are solved with creativity and imagination (do you consider yourself a person with those two skills?).

Definitively, a professional works at a personal level all of these attitudes, aptitudes and capacities («soft skills») that allow them to, in the end, make their technical work flow much better.

Guess who's the best person to work with, someone who communicates well, knows how to listen, always helps, brings ideas up constructively and know how to work in teams or someone who is just the opposite of that?

Cultivate «soft skills» as part of your personal and professional growth.

{ #13 - Comment the essential }

—

A code that has to be accompanied with a great amount of comments, is probably a code that is very hard to understand. If it was easy, it would not need to be explained through comments.

We have to write software that is as self-describing as possible, and turn to the inclusion of comments or notes as less as we can and being very precise when doing so. The best way to understand a piece of code is... reading it.

This is like taking an Ikea furniture piece out of the box and finding the 20-pages long assembly guide, you instantly know it won't be as trivial as you thought.

There are ways to write information and making the code understandable «from the same code»: choosing the correct names for the variables, classes and methods, creating functions with an appropriate name and that make a specific calculi but that is not that easy to understand at first, always making classes that are rather small and with very bounded functionality, and, of course, run tests.

That is, because implementing tests not only serves to make sure the software functions correctly (at least, all the things that have been proved), but also serve as a way to keep record of some certain functionality.

What is what the method does, exactly? You go to the associated tests and will understand quickly.

It gets worse when instead of comments you find dead code isolated with the same symbols used in your environment to create comments. You ask yourself if that code piece is really important, and what does it do there, if it was a mistake.

Do not leave commented dead code, and try to write the fewer possible comments explaining what does something.

It is only admissible the software project's own documentation (method descriptions, APIs, etc.).

Imagine you are reading a novel and over the text are the author's annotations, the highlights indicating something important, the studs, the annulated sections along with scrawl... you see it, don't you? It is exactly the same when we are talking about software.

If a code needs to be excessively commented, it means it is a hardly understandable code.

{ #14 - Take exhaustive control of your versions }

—

I'm afraid that one of the biggest problems we have as software developers is controlling what is deployed on a client, what changes will the new version suppose and trace clearly what differentiates the 2.4.3 version from the 2.5.0, for example. Even if, actually, it is just a matter of discipline and establishing with the team how such traceability work will be done.

Sometimes, a proper version management is not executed because we see it as an extra activity that puts us far from what we think is more important: adding new functionality; but, as well as test running, it is part of what we call «coding».

Recently, it is more fancied anything related to DevOps that, in a certain way, facilitate our tasks, but I'm afraid this is not the case for most companies.

Version control is a real headache if done poorly, you just have to take a look at the issues of many popular GitHub projects every time they face a big update. Not in vain, I remember a department of one company I worked for that lived in absolute chaos because they couldn't control the versions of the products (firmware of control devises) were deployed in front of the clients. Multiply the versions for dozens of projects deployed in 20 different countries and you will instantly lose your sanity.

«Configuration management» exists for something. You have to control the changes produced in a product from one version to another or the modifications an ad-hoc project will deploy in the future. Also, if necessary, you should know how to go back to a previous version (what we call «software downgrade»).

It is often ignored that this control of versions supposes an extra cost in which we should add the effort for the development of the new version or the new requisites. Try not to have it: the final cost will be higher.

Avoid problems and take care of your mental health. Perform new polished versions and with all the details. This effort will be worth it.

A great deal of the errors that we produce when updating a project, especially if it has third-party dependencies, based on a poor management of versions.

Actually, the thing is quite simple, but it demands a lot of discipline, which should run on a serious pre-production environment and keep record of each minimum change. If the company does not give you the necessary resources to do it correctly, it is your obligation to have it known. If they want you to solve the problems «red hot» (on the same pre-production environment), then you know you are taking the wrong way.

Facing any change of version, like for example, from 1.1.8 to 1.2.0, it procedurally establishes how this change affects the project that is being produced. Are there entities with data bases that should be updated? Are there third-parties that can accede to the system's API and whose behavior has changed at least minimally?

Keep records, inform and proceed with the next update posing any possible scenario.

Not keeping an exhausting version record is unprofessional.

{ #15 - With each new project, make some questions }

—

It is possible that there are no two projects that are exactly the same, but they're similar.

When you have spent some year executing projects, creating products and even playing with your personal projects, your well-digested experience will make you see patterns in many of them and develop some kind of intuition. Such intuition will allow you to see some situations and advance to some subtle problems that, without this experience, would be hard to detect.

I cannot positively demonstrate you this happens that way, but I can assure you that a professional's intuition, based on years of many different experiences, holds a great value.

A professional programmer doesn't start coding a new project from day one. As your years in the sector increase, you will learn for yourself that this is far for recommendable. I recognize that if we feel particularly motivated by a project, we feel excited to build something in our IDE as soon as we can.

However, during this initial phase, maybe sometimes the best thing is to stop for a minute to think and analyze, you can do it alone or with the team you're working with.

Which are the right technologies? We tend to use the ones we know the best and, therefore, result easier for us, but I have to keep in touch with all the options in the market.

Which architecture fits better? There is some kind of architecture for some type of projects and problems. Maybe you are not responsible for choosing the system's architecture, but having a clear propose since the beginning will be very helpful. Remember that the design as well as architecture are subject to change as the project goes on.

Can I reuse some things from similar projects? The best software companies do not start a new project from zero. If they've been smart enough, they have internally produced modules or libraries that are used on multiple projects. The result is that they are executed quicker: at a lower cost, better suitability and more happy clients because the result arrives earlier.

How has the competence or third-parties proposed a similar solution? I have conducted this analysis through many projects of my career and, as well as allowing me to learn about sectors I did not knew before, I would dare to say it help me to tune the best solution for the client. Not in vain, in 2019 I have been seeing the evolution of a corporative framework I designed myself for an aircraft manufacture company that has more than 300 employees, and I comment it just to demonstrate that such an exercise is extremely subtle and necessary.

What are the characteristics that adds more value to the client? We have to start by implementing that requirement that adds more value to the client; in that way, the related requirements will be attended first and the client will «see something important» being taking care of as soon as possible, a thing that will booth your confidence and will never let you doubt about the project's reliability.

Should I support myself on an already existent framework? Which one? Is it right to use the foundations of another software project and build upon it?

Would it be worth it to customize that similar project we did some years ago?

...

The more the development team asks these questions and others of the sort at the beginning of the project, the flatter the path will be for its development and the most likely it will be to end it successfully. Though, rectifying is something wise people do, if you take some better decisions at the beginning, the less aspects you will have to correct later, winning at productivity and suitability.

Avoid the forced excuse of the new project to finally start learning that new framework, library or environment that you have wanted to use for a while. Ask yourself if it's the right thing to do, professionally. Also, do not try to build other projects from scratch, whether they're your own or open-source, there is similar stuff you can adapt or reuse as a breaking point.

{ #16 - Use the IDE productively }

—

A programmer spends a great deal of their work hours... coding, of course, and they do it using some IDE or their preferred editor, may it be Sublime, Visual Studio Code, VI or VIM (yes, there are people who are still using those and feel happy about it), or any other one.

The thing is that we will not always know very well the editor we spend more time with and do not know how to use it productively.

Ask yourself if you deeply know the tools you use every day and if you use them in the best way possible.

We may spend many hours a week just trying to rediscover the mouse to click on this or that function (and closing, for example, the class view of the solution), when there is some keyboard shortcut to do it immediately. That same way, we may lose many minutes when we got to run unitary tests manually, when the same code editor has a function for this coding some type of script or macro.

If you do the same task multiple times and it requires «some certain time», you already have a task that is subject to automatization. Make an effort on making in systemic and save work (and life) hours.

I think that when a programmer uses their IDE right, they barely get their hands off the keyboard and barely uses the mouse. They know all the shortcuts to close help panels and just use the text editor, they know how to use the automatic refactoring utilities that all advanced IDEs have as well as its more useful extensions, they feel comfortable with the multi-cursor function, they localize archives they need with just a few key pulsations and launch the compilator or depurator from the keyboard, just to name a few examples.

I propose you this challenge: you have to change in a same archive the name of a variable X for the new more adequate name of Y: would you do it with just a few key pulsations or looking for each and everyone X appearance? That's it.

It may seem rubbish, but modern IDEs have a great deal of functions to maximize productivity, why not use them then?

Take a few minutes a day to get to know your IDE better, look for some tricks to apply; that way you will dedicate more productive time to what really matters, which is adding functionality to software and the way you work, improving some aspect of it and reinforcing its tests, among many other things.

{ #17 - Work productively }

—

This habit could be applied to any personal or professional activity, but I remind it to you because if you've never thought about how you do your job while taking care of many different tasks in record time and with minimum effort, then you have a problem you probably did not realize until now.

The most successful companies are those that «answer to the market» in a more agile and quick way, executing projects as fast as possible improving their suitability; that same way, professionals think of their time as a rather scarce resource and is always trying to optimize. If you work by yourself, doesn't it sound amazing to do things in less time?

Do you work for a company where stress is chronical and is not produced as something punctual? Do you feel like you have no time to do everything you are responsible for? That is, do you feel immersed in some sort of chaos in your daily life?

The best professional uses productivity techniques and I am really surprised this is not something we learn in our academic phase. I am also surprised some companies execute «performance tests» to their employees every once in a while, without giving them formation nor notions to improve organization or productivity.

Being productive is not working less, but better, dedicating most of your time doing the important things that actually bring some value; being productive is also doing more in less time and, therefore, our results (personal, professional, technical and economic) cannot be any better.

In the «Practical Book of the Agile Programmer» I dedicate a chapter to this important topic, also, there is some wide literature about it; however, I will give you some examples orientated to software developers.

These are just some samples of what I do myself daily, I will show them to you and hopefully, you will find them useful: I do not allow any client to use my time calling me at any time (that way I urge them to make an appointment with an appropriate agenda), I check my e-mails once or twice a day, just that, I always make previously appointed tasks (ok, let's say, 90% of them), I never accept an improvised meeting convocated hours before, I do not go to meetings without a clear agenda, I also do not let it last more than an hour and I always ask for some «actionable» conclusions, if I have some frivolous issue that only takes a few minutes to do, I do it immediately, etc.

Do you think there is some difference between using those productivity techniques and not using any? If you still do not see it, keep on reading.

Get rid of the unpleasant tasks as soon as you can, that way, you will avoid the mental purr like «uff, I still got to do this», just as we have pointed out in one of the habits in this book.

If you are «creating» new code, do it tomorrow or think of the first hours of your work day, or when you think you are more mentally clear.

Find out if you are «an owl, a lark or a hummingbird» (this is not a joke), this is, trying to find your chronotype and try to work according to it, you may be working very hard against your own biological clock and you could obtain better results if you acknowledge your own biology to be more creative. «Owls» feel more comfortable working at night, «larks» feel better working very early in the morning until noon, so «hummingbirds» (80% of the population) feel comfortable working during daytime, not so early and through the afternoon. I recommend a Begoña Pueyo book in the bibliography which is very illuminating.

If you find that you have make to make some task repeatedly, try to automatize it (executing manual tests, reports that could be automatized, etc.), or even delegate it.

Use the «pomodoro» technique for your work sessions. Resting between task and task, which increases productivity. The «pomodoro» technique («Tomato», in Italian), is a great way of working with good concentration.

Don't you ever make the error of working continuously asking yourself «what should I do next?», this is a symptom of lack of organization and planning. If you make yourself this question, then you should have your to-do list somewhere. Write at the beginning of your day (or a little bit later) a list of tasks you will do that day. Also, you can use the «ABCDE» technique to tag the importance of each one of them (and their execution order according to it).

Avoid unnecessary meetings; unproductive meetings are actual time black-holes. Generally, meetings as a way of work are overused.

Avoid distractions when you are doing a task (notifications, text messages, etc.) and try to achieve as much concentration as possible.

When you are very concentrated and get distracted by anything, you spend 15 or 20 minutes going back to the same concentration degree. Talk to your mates and have a consensus about it, for example indicating you do not want to be interrupted when your water bottle is a certain place on the table or have your headphones on (no joke). The ironic part f it is that many «managers» feel they have the right to interrupt you and, at the same time, want you to have things finished due yesterday, ignoring that with each random interruption and surely unnecessary, they cost the company some performance bucks.

Do not check you e-mails continuously, is it really necessary to check your e-mail three or four times a day?

If you find something you can do in less than two minutes, do it immediately, like reading any of the chapters of this book.

Try to plan your work not just for the day, but for the week and the month, even just generally.

Avoid people contacting you on your phone during the time in which you have to be working; remember, if you do not manage your time, others will do it for you.

Use your development environment being agile and efficient. Get some support on the tools that allow you to do your work in less time and automatize all you think you could automatize. We work with computers, if you haven't noticed yet.

Pull the string and read a good professional productivity book, like the ones I mention in the bibliography.

Who has time for their personal projects, hobbies and family? Think about it, who works productively and who doesn't?

Companies should encourage their teams to work not only with quality but productivity as well.

{ #18 - Avoid overdesigning }

There may be people who believe our job is to solve problems through code programming, but this is not true, if you haven't realized it by now with all you have read.

We have to code to solve something, but we have to do it finding the easiest and simplest solution. Why? Because any software project will be modified and evolve sooner or later and, that's why we should keep it as simple as we possibly can so it will be easier to modify and maintain.

When we code, we do not only write code lines, we also «design» (and we also build an «architecture» for it where the solution fits).

So, if we keep the code simple, the design will also be simple, elegant and readable. Not doing so would imply that the efforts you have done to write clean code with no technical debt will be obfuscated by a clumsy design that is unnecessarily complex.

Make an effort to crate designs that are also simple, so you may find useful some well-known design principles that should be part of your professional background.

I am afraid that, as in any other profession, there are programmers who show-off their knowledge by creating an unprofitable complexity. Do not do that and show-off by finding simple solutions and designs to complex problems.

A tactic for this is modulating as much as possible all the parts of the project, creating small but very concrete, readable, sustainable parts that fit in an ever-evolving architecture. The solution to a complex problem will fix itself orchestrating modules and easier parts and with concrete and homogeneous responsibilities.

You may make the mistake of creating a great architecture and design at the beginning of the project, when we still do not know that well all the requirements of it and how it will evolve in the future. It is true that there has to be some certain initial approach, but it has to be also a guide and not an iron corset where everything has to fit the functionality of a posterior stage of the project.

Do not forget that in agile development, the design keeps «emerging» as software evolves and it is continuously refactorized.

Write simple code with a structure (design) that is also as simple as possible.

On the other hand, I am surprised that even if we code with languages orientated to objects like C#, C++ or Java, barely use the fundamental concepts of object orientation (polymorphism, heritage, abstract classes, etc.). Use them as an ideal resource that could better resolve and modulate the software problems.

{ #19 - Productivize }

—

I will never get tired of repeating it: while working on a project means getting to a particular solution with a client with specific needs, creating a product is something completely different; it consists in abstracting the more general solution that could help a certain user.

Guess where is the biggest suitability? Yes, in the development of products that will not be used by one but thousands of people, and not in the development of ad-hoc projects made for a unique client.

This is viable in software and relatively easy to assume, but it requires some skills to «produce» such solution.

It is not only about adapting «something» so it can be used by some clients, it is about having an attitude to face and focus your job as a software developer.

Imagine you have to implement a library to manage a great file depository for a web app; you could implement an especial solution designed for that project, but the smart thing to do would be implementing a reusable library in many different projects (using this example because it is one of the last repositories in NPM and GitHub and it is precisely that, an archive manager, which I named «files-repo»). For some new project using Node where I have to face the usage of a great deal of archies..., using «files-repo» without a doubt, I have already «produced» such characteristic for it to be reusable for me and many other users in the Node community.

Producing is not only about selling final products to many clients, you can also produce parts of a solution.

If you are able of isolating structural parts of projects you have done so you can easily reuse them, you are walking on the right direction.

At a design level, the idea may be a little subtle to catch; think about how you got a library that serves any project and you want to publish it in GitHub so it can be used for some other project. Don't you think you would change some aspects of the library's nature? It would have to be more general, more documented and better covered with tests for a bigger version control.

You still haven't published anything? What are you waiting for? I assure you it is a great personal and professional stimulus and, you will suddenly find people in Israel, Brazil or Canada cloning and using your own software for their projects. Is there a bigger satisfaction than that?

Producing is the same as making a web for some novel writer who wants this or that, and what you do is not only the particular solution but a system where you can easily adapt (sell) the same project to many other authors.

This is a very refined version of using the same work you have done before. Guess how you can profit more from your work, if dedicating yourself to projects or producing everything you touch.

Personally, I have always felt more comfortable making products than working on projects, it is also because I know the direct contact with final clients is not always easy; let others do the talking introducing your product for them, so you can mainly focus on creating, which in my opinion or taste, is the best part and much more creative and stimulating of our profession.

Creating a product (as a framework, library or final solution), requires many more technical skills and a higher experience to execute a concrete project, so, you improve as a professional when you focus on the first rather than the last.

If you productivize a good deal of what you do, I can assure you things will get better for you.

{ #20 - Write traceable code }

—

A common problem we as developers have is to detect and solve code errors. Almost never does one write an app, not even a tiny piece of it, that is functional from the beginning; even more, when we say we «code», we actually mean is that we spend part of the time fixing mistakes. It is a core part of the software's nature.

So... errors appear, and many of them, in any of the phases of a project's lifecycle; if there is good test coverage and a QA policy going on, the number of those bugs will be reduced. However, it is almost inevitable that in production (when the project is still giving customer service), some unexpected errors leak and appear at any given moment.

What happens then? We have not prepared the solution well enough so it can give information of what has happened, which was the mistake, where and when it happened: the client will tell us that the program presents a 500 error doing this or that, or a second-realm service just stopped working. Those are typical situations.

It is so important to manage errors that even some companies launch products that aren't still mature enough to a small portion of the market so they can test them (and detect the errors, of course).

We got to introduce into the solution a good error capture policy, as well as giving it a mechanism that, if produced (and surely it will happen), we got all the proper information to purge and solve the problem as soon as possible.

If you tend to leave stuff like «try {...whatever...} catch(err) {}» in your code, then you know what I mean.

Use good and enough log strategy, in your archives as well as data bases; it is better to leave those with an information excess than lack of it.

Monitoring the long-term behavior of an app that has to work continuously, is an art in itself. Do not lose yourself on your own path, enrich the information that is registered when you produce unexpected errors.

{ #21 - Avoid a chaotic work environment }

—

You are responsible of the work environment you are surrounded by. Nobody imposes anything to you; no excuses or complaints, you just have to surround yourself with the best work circumstances and even with the best work partners that inspire you, support you and motivate you, and if you cannot achieve that, you can decide to stay there feeling unmotivated and stressed or look for something else.

I insist, nobody obligates you to anything.

As in any other creative task, dedicating a great part of your work day to being seated in front of a computer, with an open IDE, programming or purging, it demands a relatively calm environment and that inspires creation. The sad part is that many managers confuse «calm» with «working less», and it is quite the opposite. The pressure from obtaining positive results is not unmatching to being able to work in such conditions, and this demands a restful environment (at least most of the time) and a good organization.

Too many companies configurate their installations like ancient manufacturing rooms where tangible products are being produced; creating software is an activity of a different nature. Creating good software (high quality and sustainable), it demands not only good formation, but a creative environment that pleases it and a very different corporative culture. In fact, successful companies have that in common: a strong corporative culture capable of motivating their employees, like Virgin, Netflix, Microsoft, Google, etc. In those companies, many workers consider themselves fans of the companies they work for. There is certainly a reason for it.

And telling you that, you are like a plant that grows in its pot or one of those fishes that get too big for their fishbowl; in the same way, you will improve as much as your environment allows you to. Bad environments, bad professionals, open and creative environments... well that. What makes a professional who wants to grow and improve in a place where there is no room for growing? Exactly, getting out as soon as possible.

If working in a place where deadlines are decided by a non-technician (who has who knows what bidding), where the sound of telephones and conversations is constant, where creativity is only possible from nine to two and then from three to five, and where your time is at disposition of anyone who wants to interrupt you or that is at disposition of any other person who wants to book a meeting in which you may not have a lot to say, then you are fucked, I have to tell you so.

You can collect a payroll you are interested in at the end of the month, but you are professionally canned: you limit yourself and your growth. You are just on the verge of deep stress and a major motivational crisis (something that will happen more frequently as you get older). Remember: if you cannot get better, then you get worse.

If you are uncapable of changing your environment with better practices and organization, then you have to get out of it, for your sanity and your professional future.

Always remember this: you do not only work to offer a service to a third-party, your daily work is a seed that will make you a better professional (technical, manager, entrepreneur or business person).

A good professional is not only about skills, attitudes and experiences, it is also because they know the importance of working in the right place to deploy all of them.

Take a look at your last months: count the number of unnecessary interruptions you have suffered, how much unproductive meetings you have attempted where the number of «critical topics» emerged from one day to another (and you are not responsible for them). If all of this is common in your organization, you are in the wrong place: you are swallowing and suffering other people's incapacity of other to do their job. Get out of there and look for a place where objectives are clearer and you are more organized every day.

Only in a better environment you will be able to grow and improve as a professional.

{ #22 - Be an expert of how to do clean code practices and refactorings }

—

It does not matter what programming environment you use or the language and framework with which you develop your projects, if you have never been told that you have to make an effort to write code as readable as possible, then you have something important to learn.

Since more time will be spent reading, understanding and modifying existing code, it has to be written to facilitate this task. Imagine that you have to correct a text written with different typefaces, without formatting and without indentation, with cross-marks and comments above that prevent you from understanding it well. We see this same nightmare every day when we have to correct a bug or add a new feature to our project.

Clean code practices have been well known for a long time since they were mandated and described by Robert C. Martin in his book «Clean Code: A Style Guide for Agile Software Development.» Without them, without a doubt, the code that is generated is dirtier and more convoluted to understand (and therefore more expensive to modify).

Correct choice of variable names, homogeneous indentation throughout the project, small classes and methods, few lines of code, horizontal and vertical formatting and a long etcetera, are just some of the simple recommendations to apply and that they will make your software more professional.

Remember that we not only write for ourselves, but also for colleagues who will resume your work at some point, or yourself in a while when you have to remember what did this and that, so that you do not put stones in the way of your me from the future ...

It is not just a matter of writing a beautiful and easy to understand (clean) code, in addition, the design, that is, the way the code is structured and how its parts are interrelated, must also be the best possible. We not only write code but we also design it (and they are totally different aspects).

The «refactoring» practices precisely aim to improve the design of the solution, achieving, once again, improving the readability, comprehension, reusability and evolution capacity of your project.

«Extract method», «replace temp with query», «inline temp», etc., are easy-to-apply pills and recipes that when are being used over and over again, they have an accumulative effect that makes your project reach a greater professional level.

I wrote «The Practical Book of the Agile Programmer» precisely to describe the more common practices in clean code as well as «refactoring».

A professional programmer daily applies those techniques and makes an effort to see what they can do to improve the «cleaning» as well as improving the design.

{ #23 - Reuse part of your own projects }

—

Surely you have ever realized that you are implementing something the same or similar that you have previously done in another project. The implementation of an algorithm, all that common user management logic, that type of validation, those classes for the use of contexts in the same type of database, etc.

Let's be smart and don't repeat the same job more than once. Productivity is about that, working focused «creating» new things and with the least possible effort.

Although we «work», we are not paid to work, I prefer to think that we are paid to be productive and all that that entails.

«Produce» and «reuse» are two sides of the same coin.

Try to isolate the functionality that you implement in one project and that may be useful in others; Give it your own project form (library, module, framework, etc.), document it and there you will have it available later.

For this, it is necessary that you know how to program with the concept of «decoupling» in mind, that is, approach the design of the application as a set of small, isolated and independent parts that communicate and orchestrate each other to execute a specific functionality.

If you program by creating excessively monolithic (and coupled) applications, it will be difficult to extract certain functionality from them to be reused in other projects.

Curiously, if your company belongs to this niche, it is possible you will have to do some projects that are very similar for accordingly similar clients and with the same necessities. If that's so, then many of your projects will probably have things in common.

Over time, your section or company will have at tis disposition a lot of libraries and utilities to be reused on new projects and products, reducing the «time to market», the cost for the client (achieving competitivity) and increasing the profitability of everything you do.

Some companies have their own «corporative frameworks» based on the development of most of the products.

This could be the recipe for a prosper software company: using its own corporative frameworks, knowing all the technologies at their hand (even if they are scarce) and having various products to quickly adapt to new clients.

Reusing is the key.

{ #24 - Write homogeneous code }

—

There is nothing worse for a project's maintenance than finding all the classes written in a module and then written in a completely different way somewhere else.

Imagine you are reading a novel and that each chapter is written with typos and different font sizes, using an uneasy formatting and an ever-changing under lining, or literary styles that are completely opposed; with a book like that you wouldn't be able to focus and it would be hard to follow the story.

Well, this is precisely how we sometimes write the code of a project, uneven in many of its aspects.

The same thing happens when several people work on the same project; sometimes you can appreciate who did what. And this is not good, since these different styles take away the homogeneity of the solution and away from its ease of maintenance.

The code of the same solution must be homogeneous, that is: it must maintain the same type of format, it must name the variables in the same way, the spacing between one method and another must also be equal, each file must be structured in a similar way and the organization of all «assets» must also be homogeneous.

This is not a whim; it is done precisely so that it is easier for us to understand the project and locate where everything is.

For example, if you agree with the team that all the private methods are at the end of the class, then it will take less time to locate them, because you know where you will find them in all the classes of the project, if you also agree that all the constants are defined in their own project called «Constants», if each important method has a short description at the beginning, if the tests of each class and method are organized in the same way for all classes and methods, etc., it is evident that it will be much more comfortable for you to work with that code.

And that «comfort» will translate into a better efficiency, facility and time saving to advance on the project.

Creating our own style guide is something that can be done in less than an hour; the perks of this are incalculable.

As with many aspects of software, it is subtle to understand the benefit of correctly covering small details like these, and yet, along with clean code techniques, refactoring, and avoiding code smells, it all together has a cumulative effect that they make your code incomparably better than without them.

On one of the occasions when I was hired to carry out a «code audit», I found without diving too deep all the anti-practices to write maintainable code: variables declared anywhere and without homogeneous names (some were preceded by '_', others in Spanish and others in English), there were classes that were simple containers of functions with totally different functionality, there was an excess of comments everywhere, a lot of dead code (commented code), you could clearly see the hands of different people with different styles, there was nothing that smelled like «design», a lot of duplicate code, very few tests, and so on. You can imagine what a nightmare it had to be for those developers to work with that solution to which they had to continually add features (and its economic cost). Finally, in a courageous decision by the company, it was decided to start a new solution and work on a new implementation of the new system a year later.

I mean, all these good practices have a real impact on our clients and on the profitability of our work.

{ #25 - Work focused }

—

In another habit we have talked about the need to work «productively», that is, to make the most of the time available to obtain better and more results and with less effort, or what is another version of the same: to work most of the time in what we really add more value.

The psychologist Mihaly Csikszentmihalyi, a professor at the University of Claremont (California), coined the term «flow» as a state of mind in which we are so focused on a task that we forget even the concept of time. It is in those moments when we can best deploy our creativity and do the best work possible.

Detect in which activities you «flow» according to this definition and you will undoubtedly discover your passion and vocation (and therefore your talents).

There is no doubt that each person achieves those moments in those activities that they like and motivate the most. I suppose you are reading this book because you are a programmer and because it is an activity that you adore and that you have a certain vocation for it.

We must achieve the greatest number of these «flow moments» throughout our working day. Maybe each one lasts an hour or less, but it is in those periods of time where we are really concentrated.

You can't do a creative activity well (like writing, drawing, composing, programming...) without being minimally concentrated. You're getting it, right?

The mental dispersion and continuous interruptions with annihilators of creativity and those moments in which we flow with what we do.

Strive to avoid unwanted interruptions and surround yourself with an environment that you can focus on most of the time. Good professionals go bankrupt by working in a desperately chaotic, noisy environment, without organization and without the ability to foster even the slightest concentration. Curiously, many managers like to see a certain bustle in the office, as if that is how they work more ... It is true that in some more manual than mental activities, they can be done just as well without being hardly concentrated, but to program, we need to be focused most of the time, there is no more.

Not surprisingly, think of a stage in your life with a personal problem, when you had your head on it and it was difficult for you to concentrate on anything else. That stage surely did not perform in your work in the same way.

The more focused you are, the more productive you will be (and the other way around); and also, the more productive you are, the more time you will have (isn't life just made of time?). Think about all the hours you lose over the weeks and months because of stupid and unproductive interruptions.

The key to doing a better work is not working more hours, but being focused while working.

It is not easy to realize that a project carried out in an

environment where moments of relative calm and silence are not respected, where anyone feels entitled to have the time of others and where everything has to be before yesterday, It will undoubtedly be a project that will generate more costs and be of poorer quality, and, when problems arise, the finger always points to the lack of capacity of the technicians and not to an environment that can be improved so that they work more focused and concentrated and with less dispersion. Does it cost a lot to realize this?

It is your responsibility to try to work most of your concentrated time.

{ #26 - Identify the «bad smells» }

The «bad smells», also known as «code smells», those defects are well-known to make your code less readable and sustainable, favoring a worse design and, therefore, configurating a software that is more expensive to maintain. Accumulate all the «bad smells» in your solution and keep the door open to chaos, it is, a software project that is hard to maintain and evolve.

We learn by making many mistakes, although, at the same time, you realize you have been doing this or that in some way, the solution ends up being worse and they present some problems.

Those code defects are well-known and, when solving them, we get a better design with an easier code.

I bet you've come across a class with hundreds of lines of code on occasion, which implements conceptually different functionality and which you suspect is more structured. Or multiple functions that receive the same set of parameters, when not, too many parameters.

Or excessively long methods that could be synthesized with smaller methods or by creating helper classes to solve mini-problems.

What do you think will be easier to test? Classes with extraordinarily long methods or classes with smaller, more concrete methods?

Like clean code and refactoring techniques, the most common

code smells also have their own names and descriptions, such as data clumps, large class, data class, dead code, etc.

The funny thing about these techniques is that you don't need to know what the project does to realize that this and that «sucks» a bit and, therefore, is susceptible to improvement.

I insist, we do not want academic excellence in our software project, unless it is your own project with which you pursue precisely that, but what we want is a project that we deliver to a client (or many if it is a product) easy to maintain (and cheap, which is the same) and also easy to evolve (add more features or modify existing ones).

Avoid «code smells» at all costs.

{ #27 - Work in personal projects }

—

I consider myself a digital entrepreneur since 2006, when I began to carry out my first own projects in Drupal (including those of writing books, which I approach as if they were also projects). During this time, I have worked for various companies as an employee and also as a «freelance», but always, in addition to my main full-time dedication, I have always, I say, been working in parallel in my spare time on personal projects.

And I think this «extra» activity has enriched me enormously, and for that reason, I want to share what I have learned.

When you spend your time primarily for a company, chances are that you focus on the same technologies, the same types of products, and the customers are very similar.

This may be fine for those who do not have certain concerns and are comfortable doing the same type of work year after year; or it can even be great for beginners.

There may be architects who are comfortable always designing the same type of buildings, or doctors who always practice only one type of operation. However, we already know that the software industry and its related markets change at a truly astonishing speed so that with these routine dynamics we run the risk of becoming a candidate for the graveyard of technological dinosaurs.

R.I.P.

If we want to get out of our technical comfort zone, many of us have no alternative but to carry out a proof of concept from time to time with those technologies that we would like to know better, outside of your working hours or, if you are lucky and your company will It allows, dedicating a few hours a week to learn about new topics (I think there are few that have this philosophy).

Knowing something new is not a matter of reading an interesting tutorial or blog, or even reading a good book on the subject. This is fine but not enough. Without going any further, what you are reading in these pages is not going to help you if you do not practice it.

Nothing is more constructive and pedagogical than delving into a new technology when carrying out a complete project and making it available to the market. This is today more than ever viable and cheap to do, but for this you will have to dedicate time and also some euros.

Whether you have entrepreneurial concerns or not, if you want to learn about a new technology, consider a project that you think may be viable, and then take action. Knowing that you will have to make it available to users, you will take it much more seriously than a simple hobby. Although if for you it is a fun activity to pass the time, it is also good, of course, although, as I say, knowing that other users are going to see and use it, imposes a certain respect that makes your commitment greater.

Over time, this way you can also enrich your resume (you are not what you say you are, but what you show you have done) and increase your value as a professional.

There can also be an interesting side effect: some of those projects that you have undertaken can work and become part of your professional activity generating income.

I do not have any statistical study to confirm it, but the best professionals I have met (in my opinion) have always been restless people who are always busy with projects in their spare time of this and that.

Take action if you want to know something new: don't just read and inform yourself, propose a project, finish it and publish it. This is the best way to learn something in depth.

Not in vain, and I can affirm it with some pride, some of my personal projects, today, are part of my professional activity (generating income).

Commit to a project you believe in and launch it.

{ #28 - Test until you get enough and avoid «the happy path» }

A good software developer doesn't even trust their grandmother.

I mean, it knows how to program testable code (its design has nothing to do with software that does the same thing but on which it is difficult to create tests), and, furthermore, it doesn't sleep soundly without knowing that there are enough tests that show that everything works. perfectly.

The programmer with little experience, to try, usually tests what is called «the happy way», this is it, he knows what does work, and, therefore, if he does a test, that is precisely what he tests. Optimistic tests are a self-deception that sometimes reassures us because we stay calm when doing some tests, but I'm afraid they are not enough.

The professional developer takes what they had done to the limit and tests ad nauseam trying to find bugs and vulnerabilities and, for this, the same code that we have made must be embarrassed. Otherwise, you leave the seed planted so that bugs appear at the least expected moment.

In an ideal environment, there are team members with the role of testers, but I'm afraid this is less common than we would like. It is very likely that it is the same programmer who performs tests on their own code, something that is not entirely the best possible scenario. A better option is for a partner to perform tests on your code and vice versa, gaining objectivity.

Show me that your code works.

How?

Exactly, with five lines of tests for each line of productive code (this proportion is my own intuition). But with quality tests, not the ones you know will work right from the start. If you cannot maintain this proportionality, then I am afraid that your code is not testable, and therefore I recommend that you read my previous work «The Agile Programmer's Practical Book» or classics such as «Clean Code» and «Refactoring: Improving the design of existing code».

We are tempted to carry out tests that we know a priori will work. But testing is not about that, but about demonstrating that what we have developed is going to behave correctly in any situation, now and when the project evolves with more features in the future (and it sure will).

Think about it, and although you are a programmer who tests your own code as if you have a tester role, put the code you are covering to the limit and against the ropes.

Avoid the «happy path.»

{ #29 - Be an expert just from some certain areas }

—

We got the impression (and we also feel the pressure), that we need to be technological gurus to be someone in this industry.

Nothing farther from the truth.

There are those who, oblivious to the reality of our sector, think that we should know both systems administration and databases, both C # and Java or, what is worse, both Linux or Windows as well as Word and Access, also printers, networks, mobiles ... There will even be a person in charge in the company who will naively think that if you know MySql, then automatically you are also an expert in MongoDB, Oracle, etc.

Let's admit it: to be a great professional we don't need to know everything (which is impossible), but we do have to specialize in certain areas and be damned good at them.

If your thing is the administration of Oracle databases and Sql Server, go deep, put yourself in that 5% that are the best.

If you are more attracted to being a «full-stack developer», great, but don't try to know everything about all the most popular «stacks». Specialize in one and be one of the best in it.

What do you do most of your time? That is, working executing and implementing projects with the technologies you know. How much time do you spend on training? A lot less. Get it now?

And about all the other topics that you don't know anywhere near... who cares? Just try to keep abreast of current events in the sector, pecking a little here and there, reading from time to time articles, blogs or tweets, but do not make the mistake of wanting to be a great specialist (or pretend) of multitude of technologies, because, in addition to being impossible, it generates very little credibility.

I'm not saying that there are no gurus like that, of course there will be, but for the rest of us mortals (that 99.99999...%), we already have enough to enjoy with a high degree of knowledge and experience of a group of technologies counted on the fingers of hand.

I distrust (I don't know exactly why, maybe I do it instinctively) those who speak too smugly about a large group of different issues and technologies, also those companies that seem to be experts in so many others.

Today more than ever there is such a dispersion of technologies that it is inevitable that we will survive being specialists in only a small group of them. And every year new ones emerge: more services in the cloud, new stacks, new versions of frameworks, new interesting and popular third-party services, containerization, what if «blockchain», IoT, «machine learning», AI ... okay, stop.

(By the way: in my opinion, the best professional is the one who «creates» new technologies).

Doing an exercise in humility and honesty, I can say that I consider myself an expert in four technologies or areas, I know something about many others and I have no idea about the rest.

I repeat: I have no idea. It doesn't need to be. But of those four that I comment, I consider myself extraordinarily expert.

It is also not bad to be a common professional (or the heap), but it is much better to be a great professional in a particular niche, and what is not going to get you anywhere is wanting to know everything (that only naive or only the pretentious).

I still remember the time we hired a Microsoft Sql Server expert who came to our offices from Amsterdam for two days to help us on a multimillion-dollar project.

They charged us about twenty thousand euros, and their work was well worth it.

{ #30 - Read, continuously }

—

Not that long ago I read a statistic that said that in my country (Spain) it is spent about three euros more on lottery and bidding for each one on books and formation.

Whether we like it or not, we will never live from our profession doing just what we have learned on a new academic phase. One must keep on learning.

I'll say it again: we keep on learning «continuously», it is part of our profession.

It is something we go through in many other activities, between other motives because: new professions emerge!

I finished «studying» at the university in 2002, five rather difficult years in the career of Computer Engineering. You do not have to be very savvy to realize that if since then I have «lived» my profession, also passing through different roles, it has been because of a base (rather small, the one I learned before that year) and a lot of new knowledge that I have been acquiring «continuously» to this day.

Another truth that hurts: we have to get used to assuming obsolete knowledge that is no longer valid in today's world, and despite the effort or money that it will cost us to acquire it. This is part of the game. I see it like this (perhaps a little to encourage me about it): such knowledge that is no longer valid, help us to acquire other more quickly and update ourselves with less effort.

This dynamic reality is not only not going to change, but it is going to accelerate (I am not saying it, but that is what all those people and authors that I respect and who speak on the subject say).

So much so that, in essence, our activity is based on «knowing how to learn»: new techniques and technologies, new skills and even new professions.

For that reason, I am surprised by professionals who read little or nothing.

In case you don't know, reading is our best tool to get to know a topic in depth.

It is fine and it is also enriching to read blogs, listen to podcasts and watch instructional videos (I do it all the time), but this is necessary but not enough: I think that the best professional not only uses these sources, they also attend seminars or webinars (free and paid) and, of course, invest money when acquiring relevant books on the subject.

I advise you to always have a good book in your hands on any subject that interests you and in which you want to deepen. No blog is going to delve into a subject as much as in a specific book about it. What's more, most blogs implement the concept of «content marketing» as a way to attract users who eventually purchase their products, that is, they can offer quality content, but following that sales strategy, they will never offer your best content.

It also counts the readings that you take during the year. Who do you think becomes a better professional? Someone who has read fifty books in the past year or who has not read any?

Don't you think that the first one, after the years, will be an infinitely better and more demanded professional?

Today more than ever we have options to read on any subject and at affordable prices. I go everywhere with my Kindle, and still today I wonder how it took me so long to buy it (in fact, this is the second I have).

Think of it this way: reading is part of your job. Point. If it is true that everything is already written, you just have to correctly locate what you still have to learn. When you have a problem, then it is that you have not yet found the proper reading. Look at it that way.

Nothing has been so enriching for me and as a reason for personal and professional change as all the readings accumulated over so many years.

This is another pattern that I have discovered for myself: the best professionals read, a lot, about the subjects in which they consider themselves «good professionals.»

{ #31 - Start with the things that add value }

—

Undoubtedly that is what software developers do: add value to others, or what is the same, create a useful solution with which we solve a problem for a client. In essence, like any professional activity, we solve problems.

If you look at it this way, our profession is not really about «programming» (or any related activity), but about «solving problems for clients», and for this we «program», so that the more problems you solve, the more clients you solve, the better. Things will go you and your professional career will shine more.

When we start a project, we often forget this point of view, so we are easily tempted to start implementing residual parts of the solution but are more attracted to it, rather than putting all the weight initially on it. What else will the end customer value; There are even those who play on a whim with what they «cool» the most. This should not happen in an organization that uses some kind of methodology to order the development phases and the implementation of features.

Quickly give the customer what they need most, save the trivial and other details for later; If the customer is new, this will multiply their trust in you tenfold, because you are soon delivering something that they value very much. Think about the opposite, that months and months go by in which the client only sees progress in areas that are relevant but not the most important;

then your perception of the project will be different and you will start to get nervous.

The same thing happens if you work on a personal or entrepreneurial project. At the time of writing this, I have founded «Hub de Libros» (www.hubdelibros.com) and we are clear that the first great functionality, the one that adds the most value, is that authors can easily create their author pages (guess at where we are putting all efforts initially).

Establish the foundations of the project and whether you are the project manager or a developer with the ability to decide what to implement in the first place, always choose what you perceive as most important for the client and deliver it as soon as possible.

{ #32 - Do not encourage knowledge islands }

—

This is a pattern that, unfortunately, I have come across often and that I think does a lot of damage in our sector, that is why I include it as a habit (rather an anti-habit).

There are those who are tempted to think that if they are the only people who dominate something in particular in the company or in the department, the only people who understand about that essential topic or the only people that the company can turn to when solving such problem, then they are assured of a job (they have hidden themselves in it and, without realizing it, are digging their own professional grave).

These people are far from knowing the least all those «soft skills» that I have talked about earlier.

And they are also insecure people with very low self-esteem, I'm afraid.

The security of a good professional is not in appropriating for yourself something that no one else in your organization can do, believing that this way you will keep your position, your status or whatever it is for life. Authentic security consists in knowing that you can solve problems because your skills and attitudes allow it, nothing more, so that the good professional does not shy away from new challenges (which always come disguised as problems) but rather face them with the energy of personal growth.

Appropriating an island of knowledge, in addition to being petty, makes you weak, because it is preventing you from growing professionally and, believe me, anyone will end up dominating what you want to protect unless they set their mind to it.

I fell into this error once (long ago, huh!), And I actually talk about this episode in «The Black Book of the Programmer.» Outcome? I realized that «being the only one who knew how to do this» was blocking me on the corporate ladder and limiting my growth. I took note and reacted in time.

Seen from another angle, if you have responsibilities over a team, it prevents islands of knowledge from existing, it is a risk that can take its toll on you and your organization.

{ #33 - Read projects made by others }

—

Reading a few articles on a topic that interests you, even buying a book and reading it to you from start to finish in a weekend, watching a couple of videos from someone from Google who also talks about that topic, is very good. In fact, it is fantastic and necessary.

But it is even better and it is a step further, to see how others have implemented a real project on GitHub or other similar public repositories.

I admit that I have learned a lot by snooping projects on GitHub, especially Node, analyzing how the authors have raised this and that, so that, in the end, for many details I have ended up copying all those good practices that I have seen that the «community» who knows more than I do on the subject.

Seeing a software project created by someone else is the most enriching thing for me, it's like learning by reverse engineering.

Exactly the same thing happens in literature: learning to write better by reading who we consider to be the best authors or who we want to emulate. In software it is the same, we learn by reading the work of others.

It is also true that you find yourself in everything as well as half projects, without tests and poorly planned, something that, if you think about it, also serves to develop that sense of what can be improved.

Choose any topic that interests you, for example «image recognition», search GitHub and immediately start learning about things related to that concept (libraries, third-party services, reference articles, etc.).

And it also happens the other way around: publish a project yourself and wait for them to point out defects («issues») and improvements (another way to learn), and even request the inclusion of changes because someone wants to use them.

{ #34 - Always work with planned tasks }

—

I know. The environment where you work is in chaos, your boss tells you that this new task has to be completed by the day before yesterday, suddenly you are called for an impromptu meeting and you have a heavy client on the phone who calls you three times every day.

Whether your work dynamic is similar to the previous one or not (I hope you don't feel too identified), a good professional has to work in a minimally organized environment.

And planned.

The roles and responsibilities, the priorities and the way of working are organized, but the concrete tasks that derive from all the above are «planned».

A planning is given by a specific objective, a person in charge, and an end date. Nothing else is needed.

Surely you are not responsible for establishing this planning in your organization; If it doesn't exist, you have problems, and serious ones, and if you have the ability to create a planning and you don't do it, too.

Planning any job is like having a budget: you include those items that you give priority to before others.

Extrapolating this concept... Do you spend more on outings than on food for the home? Does your golf club cost you more than extraordinary tasks or your children's school? The budget will reveal it to you.

It is the same with planning; If it is not done, then the clear exercise of «what is the most important thing for the company in the next few days» is not carried out. If you are freelance and work for yourself, remember that you are «your own company.»

Planning is to discern between what is important, what is urgent and what is less relevant and schedule it in time.

Without minimal planning, there is only one possible scenario: chaos. Decide if you want to live in it or in an environment with clear priorities and well-defined objectives.

Some live well in unorganized environments (where it is more difficult to take responsibility when problems explode), but good professionals know that a good job can only be done when it is under the umbrella of good planning.

The same on a personal level: plan your day, indicate the tasks that you are going to carry out and go crossing them one after another.

Productivity is ensured by taking a step back, analyzing priorities and determining the tasks and their order to be carried out during the next day or week.

Try that almost everything you do, has been planned previously; this will multiply your results.

{ #35 - Think and work for the client }

—

In another habit, I have commented on the need to start with what adds the most value to your client. That is important and necessary, although not sufficient.

A good professional does not do what he likes best in a project (even if it is not of real use to the client), he does not even always do «everything» that the client thinks he needs.

We have to put ourselves in the shoes of the client, know their business as well as possible, even detect needs that they have and that they do not realize.

That is, the client is not always clear about the problems they have to solve, they need us more than we think to correctly determine what they really need. Think about it.

In an ideal environment, there is a functional analyst or a «product owner» who constitute roles that must perform this task, but it is possible that you work on your own and you are the one who is in direct contact with the client.

Helping a client is not only about implementing the project that they have specified better or worse, it is putting yourself in their place, knowing them well and proposing solutions that may be far from their initial plans. This attitude is the one that must be maintained not only at the beginning of the project, but throughout it.

Do it like this and I assure you that you will have the trust of your client in a short time, because they will no longer see you as a supplier to entrust a job of any kind, but as a thinking part of their organization that seeks to solve problems.

I love hiring someone for any kind of job and being surprised by giving me a better solution than I would have ever thought of. Who do you think I will call again when I have another similar problem? Who am I going to give positive references to? Guess it. Exact.

Wear your client's suit, understand it and thus you will retain not only the work of now, but that of the future.

{ #36 - Invest in your formation }

—

We have already commented on another habit the importance of reading as part of our professional activity.

Never in history has it been so cheap to learn, so much so that information is more accessible than ever and its format is presented in all possible ways (videos, texts, audios, subscriptions, etc.). Not surprisingly, «content marketing» is one more tool for commercial attraction: I teach you something in exchange for your interest in my products.

On the other hand, I think that, sometimes, really good content or courses that can save you many hours and a lot of reading, are not free, so we can choose to spend (invest) in them if we want more and better results (and before).

That is, we must have a budget for training. Whether it is in the purchase of MOOCs, face-to-face seminars, regulated and approved courses, masters or certifications, dedicating part of your income to continue training can be your best investment.

I admit that I am educated mainly by reading books, but I also spend several hundred euros a year on paid training (and I think it may be little), depending on my availability and the topics I am interested in at all times, but I know I have I have to dedicate part of my budget to that area. I'm also a Packt Publishing subscriber and I think it's the best money I can spend on.

Think about it: wouldn't it be surprising if we spend more money on beers with colleagues than on your own training? It is a question of priorities, and also of finding a certain balance.

As a good Spaniard, I like a beer in my neighborhood bar, but as a good professional, I dedicate much more budget to my continuous training as a professional.

{ #37 - Apply continuous improvements }

—

«If you do not get better, then you are getting worse». But don't panic, this vital principle should not give you excessive stress.

I am a great follower of continuous improvement, both personally and professionally; It is not that I am obsessed, nor do I seek an unhealthy perfectionism in everything, far from it, but I do understand that wanting to continually improve is a positive and enriching attitude in all areas of life.

I understood long ago that perfection is nothing more than a utopia whose sole purpose is to point us in the direction to follow.

Sometimes we wonder how such a person has been able to get to what they are today, or how such a company is achieving the results we admire. Or quite the opposite: how that friend from college ended up so badly, in any sense, drunk and out of work (it's just a somewhat extreme example).

There is only one answer: little by little.

Nurture a continuous spirit of improving every day, just one aspect, even if it is small and insignificant.

The important thing is to have that conscious attitude of improvement; and the pace does not matter, but the direction.

I recognize that writing a book, like this one, is not an easy task and requires many hours of dedication and even documentation that, in addition, I make compatible with many other activities, not even talking about domestic and family matters.

I also acknowledge that it does not have too much merit: just a little discipline and a personal commitment to finish it on that date and carry out up to five comprehensive reviews of the text. This translates into many tasks, many, that I myself plan in my Wunderlist (a very simple task management web app).

And how do I do it? You already know, little by little; Today one hour, on the weekend maybe two, that Friday afternoon when I have a little more time, maybe four, but always like this, every day one step forward even if it is only a few centimeters.

Continuous improvement is about that. In advancing at the rate you can, in the matters that interest you, but advancing at the end of the day.

It is not about improving «just because», you also have to be clear about the direction, the ultimate goal.

Do you want to be a technical writer in two years? Do you want to work as an AI expert? Do you want to run the next marathon in your city?

Then you know how: having the destination clear, you just need to get going.

Every day a little. But «every day.» You can't imagine the power that exists in dedicating every day even a few minutes to what motivates you.

Okay, we already know that we improve in steps, but how do we verify that this is the case? For a few years I have been keeping an exhaustive accounting of the aspects of my life that interest me the most and in which I think I should work to grow and improve: from my own personal care practicing yoga, running, etc., to attending webinars, readings, my own finances and completed projects. Every now and then I look back and compare where I was on those issues twelve months ago and where I am now.

Improving, whatever this means to you, is not a whim but a necessity in a society with a changing and dynamic economy.

{ #38 - Take care of the details }

—

«As you do something, so you do everything.» I have read this phrase on several occasions and I think it contains the essence of how we project who we are in everything we do in life, both personally and professionally.

There is even a book out there that claims that the best professionals start the day with a clear and strong routine from the moment they get out of bed (they stop for a few minutes to do it with all the care in the world).

I am afraid that there are those who in the work environment show a personality and in other environments (friends, family) another totally different. Perhaps in hostile environments where the corporate ladder is only climbed by kicking colleagues, this makes sense.

I got out of that dynamic years ago and there is not a day that goes by that I am not happy about it.

We cannot be different people in our personal and professional activity; Or what is the same, if you are a meticulous person, you will be with your partner, your house and also in your work.

The best professionals are detail-oriented in many aspects of their lives and they care down to the last detail.

Moreover, when faced with offers from similar competitors, a client will always opt for the one that stands out with those small details: a better presented budget, a technical offer with better design and better graphics, etc.

I have verified it in first person: a technical proposal presented with great rigor but also in a well-edited document, with a good design, clear, concise and even attractive, ended up giving very good results. Would it have been the same if you had presented it in a simple email? Not at all, those design details and well-worked contents clearly decided the result.

There will always be the exceptions that prove the rule: geniuses with disastrous personal and domestic lives, and others who like to live in a house that is orderly to the pathological while working at a cluttered and littered desk. I dare say that this profile is just something residual.

In the end, we distinguish ourselves in many orders from our competition (other companies or other professionals of the same level), for small details.

That API a little better documented, those «a little» better-crafted examples, that somewhat better-worded email, that response sent a little earlier.

Take care of the details, and they will make sure to hang you the certificate of the best professional.

{ #39 - Learn how to be criticized }

—

When I published the first version of «The Black Book of the Programmer» in 2014 (after having written many other things but not having published any), I was looking forward to the first «reviews» on Amazon. When they arrived, if they were good, they made my day, but if they were not, they left me a little wrecked. Fortunately, and after several years and more than a hundred comments, the majority are positive.

Exactly the same has happened with the rest of my books and my two novels.

And exactly the same has happened when I have presented to a multitude of clients products in which I have participated (and that I think are excellent): some of them liked it a lot, but, with a few others, you feel as if they had given you a kick in the pit of the stomach.

Over the years I have learned that criticism is inherent to whatever you do and that you «expose» to a relatively wide audience.

However, that possibility of being criticized, keeps many away from developing their talents and exposing them to the fullest. Don't let this happen to you.

Whether what you do is good or not, you can always have malicious critics: in your repositories on GitHub, on your personal blog, in your work environment if you start to stand out, etc.

You will find good critics (those who help you grow and improve, always contributing something constructive) and bad critics (who try to hurt you personally and tear your work down out of sheer envy).

Attend to the former, and ignore the latter.

I know this takes a while to sink in, but when you become a good professional, you end up accepting it.

Use helpful criticism from others as a source of information to improve.

The better professional you are, the more you are going to pose a threat just by your presence to other mediocre «professionals». This is an unquestionable human reality. Learn to cope with it and also learn that it is a small price that you must pay for your personal and professional development.

Observe who criticizes you in an excessive and unjustified way, you will see for yourself that they are almost always people who, deep down, are saying to themselves something like «Damn, I'm not like this uncle (aunt) and I'm far from being or to do what it is and what it does.»

Don't let destructive criticism ruin you, go your way even if not everyone likes you. Not even your mother-in-law.

Also forget the need to please everyone, because both that and avoid receiving criticism at some point, it is simply impossible.

Use constructive criticism as one more tool with which to improve.

{ Finishing }

—

I consider myself a professional programmer and I have lived from this activity for more years than I remember. As you have seen, this book not only talks about software, how to create better code, without going into great technical considerations, but also focuses on the habits that I consider make a good professional.

I bet there are other routines, attitudes and habits that make us even better professionals, but I have selected all of the above for two reasons: the first because, personally, I value them more than others, and the second because many of them are broad topics in themselves so I encourage you to delve into them looking for additional and specific material (such as everything related to «soft skills», refactoring, etc.). In the bibliography you have a wide reference.

Read the title of each section again, from beginning to end, and think if you will not be a better professional if you incorporate most of those attitudes and habits into your life.

As I have read on occasions: «there is no professional development without personal development», and from that concept emanates what I have wanted to convey in the previous pages.

A technical job is not just a technical job, behind there are a series of conditions, cognitive abilities, organization and even a way of learning and improving that determine the result of that same job.

Nothing is more gratifying for me than knowing that this short job has helped you to improve some aspect of your profession and that you are more encouraged than ever to continue working hard and get closer every day to the best professional you can become.

You can count on me at contact@rafablanes.com as well as ask me to give a talk or seminar in your organization about the books already published and topics that I discuss on my personal website, nothing would make me more excited.

Let me ask you one last favor: if you think that the pages of this short book that I have written with so much love and thought on my part, have helped you in any way, I would appreciate a positive comment on the platform where you have acquired it, so that so this information can reach more people.

Thank you for joining me here and we continue to see each other at www.rafablanes.com.

Rafael Gómez Blanes
Seville (Spain), October 2020

{ The Author }

—

Business man, software developer from more than I can remember, I own a company (Blanes Media and Technology SL). I am currently working as a consultor and software development director at Solid Stack (www.solidstack.es), a company where we try to establish a development paradigm based on good practices through a good work environment and, above all, quality products that makes us establish long-term relationships with our clients.

I graduated as a Compute Science Engineer from the University of Seville (Spain) on 2000. Since then I have gone through various work and professional experiences and have found many different technologies that would became obsolete before the predicted time.

I am also undertaking many personal projects from different natures, like Picly.io, Green Kiwi Games and, more recently, my favorite project: www.hubdelibros.com.

I share my professional and corporative experience through writing using technical articles that I publish on www.rafaelblanes.com and Medium, I have also published some novels under the pseudonym of G. Blanes (like «Patricia», «The Triplets and the Writing Club», and there are more on the way).

In 2014 I published «The Black Book of the Programmer», with a revision in 2017, and that frequently ranks as number one in sales on Amazon within its category; In 2019 I finished «The Agile Programmer's Practical Book», a practical answer to the first, as well as «The Lean MP Method», a way of systematizing the procedural implementation of business and entrepreneurial activities.

Of the companies I have worked for, not many, to tell the truth, Telvent Energía (now owned by the French Schneider Electric) profoundly marked my professional development. Thanks to this company, I was able to participate in projects of many types: national and international, R + D + i, prototype development, touching very diverse technologies. From C ++ until we adopted the first version of the .NET framework (no more memory gaps !!!). I was able to work sometimes scheduling twelve hours a day and even weekends when milestones were tightening. I also had the opportunity to participate in various work teams, some of them international.

I was displaced in Sweden in 2006 for a year and a half on a project for an electricity company, which allowed me to see first-hand a different work culture (apart from being fed up with cinnamon rolls, meat balls and being very cold). Both I and my colleagues suffered many crises in Gothenburg in the project for which we were working, but we went through them all until we had a great experience that we now all remember fondly. If you have to get out of «your comfort zone» in order to progress, then I already think I got out of it, and a lot at that time, until it became almost a habit for me to this day.

Based on my Swedish experience, I began to lead small work teams in which I completely decided the architecture and design (and I do not say it with pride, on the contrary, that role comes with a great responsibility), and also the most relevant of the developments. I also began to participate in the writing of tenders and to travel to many parts of the world including the Microsoft offices in Seattle, and I also began to take an interest in everything related to the culture of open source and agile development and try to implement it in the company I worked for. It was then when my first experiences as a freelancer, entrepreneur and external consultor began and I tried to make them compatible with my work duties.

By 2010/2011 I felt that I needed a complete change of direction in my professional career, so the opportunity presented itself shortly after. In 2012 I directed the creation for Telecontrol STM (a company closely linked to the electricity sector in my country) of an office dedicated exclusively to software development, with sufficient resources, time and equipment to develop the IRIS Remote Management Platform, a product that today Today it is working successfully in different countries: single product, same version, in different facilities with their particularities and using the concept of «Inversion of Control» a lot to achieve this.

Since then, all my activity has been dedicated to the development of products (more than projects that begin and end for final clients) and the undertaking of projects that are as scalable as possible, with greater or lesser success, trying to influence all good practices that I detail in this work.

In 2017 we decided to carry out a re-branding process and found a software company called Solid Stack in what was the Telecontrol STM software division so that we were not so tied to the electricity sector.

Hand in hand with «lean» methodologies, at the beginning of 2018 we launched a great project of which I am currently very proud and which I started myself by making a simple prototype (MVP or «minimum viable product»); As I have indicated before, it is Picly, an image server on the fly, a real development challenge because it is a certainly complex product, as well as organizational and management. Picly is made in Node and uses Redis as its database. At Picly, we use the Lean MP method for its management.

In the same way, in recent years I have been hired to give some talks as well as to give seminars related to clean code, refactoring, agile software, testing and quality audits of projects, surprising me again at the alarming lack of this culture in professional environments.

You can find some of my code repositories at github.com/gomezbl and you can definitely contact me at contact@rafablanes.com.

A tireless reader, yoga and running practitioner, father of two wonderful girls who try not to get too interested in software development ...

I am at your disposal at www.rafablanes.com or at Upwork.com

{ Bibliography }

"Code Complete: A practical handbook of software construction", by Steve McConnel.

"Clean Code: A Handbook of Agile Software Craftmanship", by Robert C. Martin.

"Culture Decks Decoded: Transform your culture into a visible, conscious and tangible assset", by Bretton Putter

"Delegation & Supervision", by Brian Tracy.

"The Money Code", by Raimón Samsó.

"The Lean Entrepreneur Book", by Brant Cooper & Patrick Vlaskovits.

"El Libro Negro del Emprendedor", by Fernando Trias de Bes.

"The Black Book of the Programmer", by Rafael Gómez Blanes.

"El Libro Práctico del Programador Ágil", by Rafael Gómez Blanes.

"The Lean Startup: How Today's Entrepreneurs Use Continuous Innovation to Create Radically Successful Businesses", by Eric Ries.

"The Power of Habit: Why We Do What We Do in Life and Business", by Charles Duhigg.

"The Sorites Principle", by Ian Gibbs.

"La Era de los Expertos", by Raimón Samsó.

"Lean Analytics: Use Data to Build a Better Startup Faster", by Alistair Croll.

"Libertad Financiera: Los cinco pasos para que el dinero deje de ser un problema", by Sergio Fernández.

"Los hábitos cotidianos de las personas que triunfan: ¿Eres búho, alondra o colibrí?", by Begoña Pueyo.

"The 7 Habits of Highly Effective People", by Stephen R. Covey.

"Mind Mappin", by Tony Buzan.

"Misión Emprender", by Sergio Fernández & Raimón Samsó.

"Móntatelo Por Internet: Cómo Emprender Tus Negocios Online, Ganar Dinero por Internet y Vivir La Vida Que Sueñas", by Victor Espig.

"Getting Things Done", by David Allen.

"Design Patterns", by Erich Gamma.

"Planifica Tu Éxito, De Aprendiz A Empresario", by Roberto Canales Mora.

"Pomodoro Technique Illustrated", by Staffan Noteberg.

"Refactoring: Improving the design of existing code", by Martin Fowler & Kent Beck.

"Running Lean", by Ash Maurya.

"Soft Skills: The software developer's life manual", by John Sonmez.

"Start Small, Stay Small: A Developer's Guide to Launching a Startup", by Rob Walling.

"The Agile Samurai: How Agile Masters Deliver Great Software", by Jonathan Rasmusson.

"The Clean Coder: A code of conduct for professional programmer", by Robert C. Martin.

"The Nature of Software Development: Keep it simple, keep it valuable, build it piece by piece", by Ron Jeffries.

"The Pommodoro Technique", by Francesco Cirillo.

"The Pragmatic Programmer", by Andrew Hunt.

"Vivir con abundancia", by Sergio Fernández.

"Vivir sin jefe", by Sergio Fernández.

"100€ startup", by Chris Guillebeau.

{ Other works by Rafael Gómez Blanes }

—

The Black Book of the Programmer_

In 2014 I published the first edition of The Programmer's Black Book, with a second revised version in 2017. In that first work, I indicated all those bad practices that make a software project end in failure, from bad group dynamics and lack of from methodology to why the «technical debt» occurs.

In a way, The Agile Programmer's Practical Book is the technical version of that first book that has been so well received over the years.

It can be purchased on Amazon and Google Play.

The Practical Book of the Agile Programmer_

(Spanish edition). An introduction to the complete software development cycle from an agile approach. This book brings together the most common clean code practices, refactoring, design principles, testing, and configuration management, along with reflections on the creative and artistic nature of software and productivity techniques for developers. If you liked The Programmer's Black Book, in this new work by Rafael Gómez Blanes, you will find the essential keys for any professional programmer, with dozens of examples taken from real projects in C # and Javascript. With a presentation by Aurelio Gandarillas, expert in software testing and quality.

The Lean MP Method

(Spanish edition). Developing an entrepreneurial project, digital or not, is an exciting, creative activity and the door to position yourself as the best professional, improve your income and grow. But ... what happens once you have made your project available to users? Sales never come alone. Post-launch management is equal to or more important than the solution, product, or service you offer. Following the «lean» methodology, with the Lean MP method and its Matrix of Procedures, you have a simple, practical and agile way to manage, control and improve all aspects of your business, without the need for a renowned MBA or hiring a billionaire CEO.

Aprende a emprender

El método Lean MP

Gestiona tu proyecto emprendedor de forma sencilla,
simple y eficaz mediante la Matriz de Procedimientos

RAFAEL GÓMEZ BLANES

Autor de El Libro Negro del Programador
y El Libro Práctico del Programador Ágil

Ediciones BMT